# Explore Colonial America!

VERNA FISHER

ILLUSTRATED BY BRYAN STONE

To Chloe, Jack, and Sam who make me feel young, but make sure I don't forget my age. And to Nick who fills my life with music.

# green press

## INITIATIVE

Nomad Press is committed to preserving ancient forests and natural resources. We elected to print Explore the Solar System! on 30% post consumer recycled paper, processed chlorine free. As a result, for this printing, we have saved:

7 Trees (40' tall and 6-8" diameter)

2,531 Gallons of Wastewater

5 million BTU's of Total Energy

325 Pounds of Solid Waste

610 Pounds of Greenhouse Gases

Nomad Press made this paper choice because our printer, Thomson-Shore, Inc., is a member of Green Press Initiative, a nonprofit program dedicated to supporting authors, publishers, and suppliers in their efforts to reduce their use of fiber obtained from endangered forests.

For more information, visit www.greenpressinitiative.org.

Environmental impact estimates were made using the Environmental Defense Paper Calculator. For more information visit: www.papercalculator.org.

"This logo identifies paper that meets the standards of the Forest Stewardship Council. FSC is widely regarded as the best practice in forest management, ensuring the highest protections for forests and indigenous peoples."

# Contents

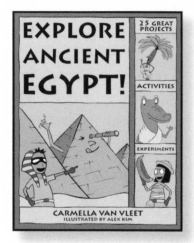

# Let's Explore
# Colonial America!

**H**ave you ever been on a camping trip? Or have you ever traveled on a ship? Do you know what it's like to move to a new place? Well, the **colonists** did all of those things when they traveled to America.

So, where was **colonial America**? What was it like to live in colonial America over 300 years ago, and where did the **settlers** come from? We'll find the answers to these questions and have fun along the way. In this book you will learn about homes, food, games, and famous people like Pocahontas. There will be lots of activities, silly jokes, and fun facts too. You will be able to make soap boats, candles, pancakes, muffins, and plenty more. Are you ready to have fun? Okay, then let's explore!

# COOL ARTIFACT

Did you ever wonder why we call this country America? Well, a mapmaker heard that Amerigo Vespucci had found the New World. Amerigo Vespucci was an explorer from Italy. The mapmaker put the name America on many maps of the **New World**. Later some people wanted the name changed, but it was too late by then because the name was very popular.

## Who Were the Settlers and Why Did They Come?

Spanish, Dutch, French, and British settlers came to this country. People wanted to move here for many reasons. Some came for the adventure of sailing on the seas. Some came hoping that they would become rich.

WORDS TO KNOW

**colonist:** a person who came to settle America.

**colonial America:** the name given to this country when talking about the years 1607–1776.

**settlers:** the men, women, and children who came from other countries to settle in the New World.

**New World:** what is now America. It was called the New World by people from Europe because it was new to them.

**colonies:** early settlements in America.

**American Revolution:** the war fought by the colonists for freedom from Great Britain.

Many British people came so they could believe in what they wanted. Religion was very important to many colonists. It was a part of their everyday life. They could be building houses, working in the garden, or getting the children ready for bed. It didn't matter.

Everything they did was about following the teachings of the Bible.

All of the settlers were brave for traveling by ship. Men, women and children traveled to this new land. The trip was hard and took many weeks.

## When Did All of This Happen?

The first British **colony** was called Jamestown. It began in 1607 in Virginia. The years we will explore are called the colonial period. That is from 1607 to 1776. Mostly this book will talk about British settlers and colonies, but we will learn about settlers from other countries too.

## THEN & NOW

Traveling over oceans could only be done by ship. : Today most people fly over oceans in airplanes.

Virginia
-1607-

Jamestown

# Color a Map of the 13 COLONIES

Colonial America was the name given to the 13 settlements founded in what is now the United States. These settlements were called colonies. They were all along the East Coast of the United States. With time the colonies grew larger and they became states after the **American Revolution.**

Do you know the names of those 13 colonies? They were Virginia, Massachusetts, New York, New Hampshire, Maryland, Connecticut, Rhode Island, Delaware, North Carolina, South Carolina, New Jersey, Pennsylvania, and Georgia. This is the order they were settled. New York was originally a Dutch colony called New Netherland, but the British took it over and renamed it in 1664.

The 13 colonies were founded between 1607 and 1733. Each colony was very different. In the north it was very cold in the winter. In the south it was very hot in the summer. Many settlers were not used to this weather.

**Georgia was the last of the colonies to be founded. It was established in 1733.**

**H**ere is a map of the 13 colonies to color. If you lived in those days where would you like to live?

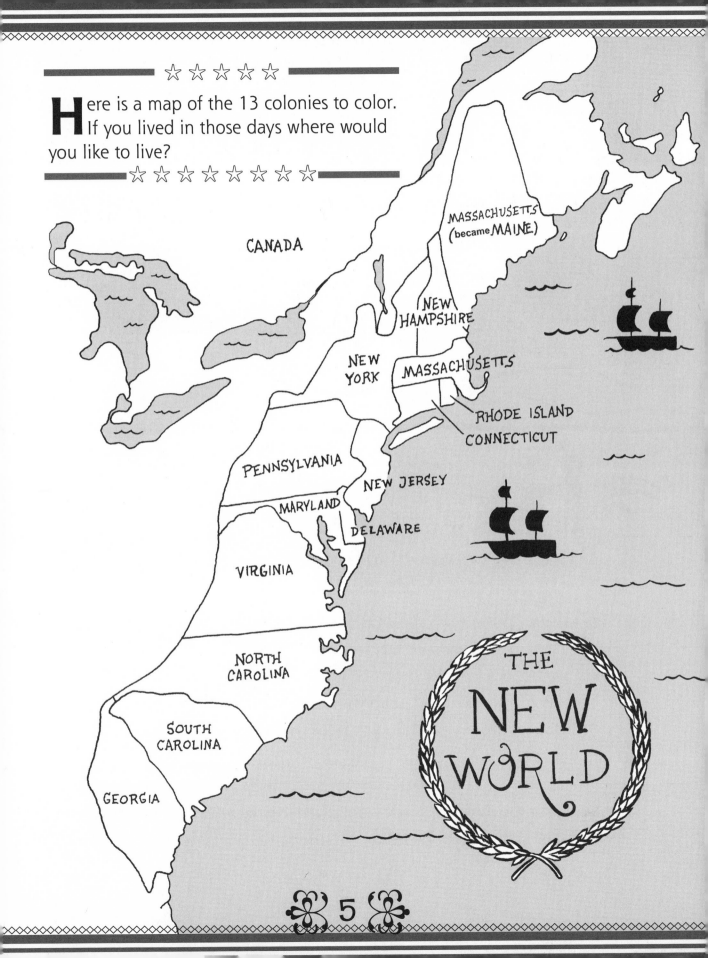

CANADA

MASSACHUSETTS (became MAINE)

NEW HAMPSHIRE

NEW YORK

MASSACHUSETTS

RHODE ISLAND

CONNECTICUT

PENNSYLVANIA

NEW JERSEY

MARYLAND

DELAWARE

VIRGINIA

NORTH CAROLINA

SOUTH CAROLINA

GEORGIA

THE NEW WORLD

# Homes
## Yours or Mine?

**H**ave you ever seen a picture of a forest or walked in one? A **forest** is an area with lots of trees. Birds, rabbits, frogs, foxes, bugs, and bears live in a forest.

———◆●◆———

Well, when people from Europe started coming to America there were no familiar roads or houses, no stores, and no churches. The land was beautiful, but much of it was vast forest and wilderness! The Native People used pathways and waterways to get around. Their houses were very different from the houses the colonists had left behind.

The first colonists in colonial America came from England. They had traveled by ship for many weeks. While they must have been very happy to be on land, they were tired and hungry, and needed shelter.

## Unsolved Mystery—The Lost Colony

The very first attempt to settle in America was made in Roanoke, Virginia, in 1587. A man named John White was in charge. He went back to England to get supplies for the people in Virginia. On the way his ship ran into some bad weather. Then war in England kept him from getting back to Virginia quickly.

When he finally returned to Roanoke in 1590, everyone had disappeared. He did find two messages, though. The messages were "Cro" and "Croatan." The first word was carved onto a tree. The second word was carved into a fence pole. It was the name of an island near Roanoke. John White searched, but never found the people.

Experts believe the 117 settlers ran out of food. They may have moved to look for food. They may have died. No one knows what happened to the people of the Lost Colony. It is still a mystery.

They built a settlement called Jamestown, Virginia, in 1607. Do you think they were surprised that they had to build a place to sleep after such a long time at sea?

The Jamestown colonists were not very prepared to build a house. They did not have

**forest:** an area with lots of trees and wildlife.

the right tools. Many did not even know the first thing about building a house. So, what do you think they did? They made the best shelter they could with what they had. Some may have made a kind of tent, whiles others were able to build small, one-room homes.

## Massachusetts

Boston

In Massachusetts the colonists may have dug into the sides of hills to make their huts strong. Next, they would cut down some trees for logs. They would make posts and beams out of the logs and stand the posts straight up.

They wove branches and sticks, called **wattle**, in the spaces between the posts. Mud, called **daub**, covered the wattle. The mud kept the wind and rain out. Finally, they used beams to make a roof. It was hard work to build a house. The colonists worked together, and children helped with the work too.

If you were a colonist which job would you like? Would you like to dig, spread the mud between the posts and beams, or yell "timber" while the trees were falling?

Many **Native Americans** lived in **wigwam** homes. These homes could be built quickly. They used bark coverings over poles forming a dome shape. The ground acted as the floor. This kind of home was a good shelter.

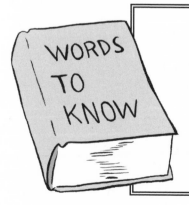

WORDS TO KNOW

**wattle:** sticks and straw filling the spaces between logs.

**daub:** clay mixture used to cover the wattle in between logs in colonial houses.

**Native Americans:** the native people who already lived in areas settled by the colonists.

**wigwam:** a dome-shaped house made with bark covering a frame of saplings.

**veranda:** a large porch with a roof above it.

**Q:** How many colonists does it take to screw in a light bulb?

**A:** None. There weren't any light bulbs back then.

As time went on the colonists were able to build larger houses. Different styles were used in different times and places. Swedish colonists built log cabins. These homes used rounded logs that were stacked on top of each other. The ends had chunks cut out so the logs locked into place at the corners. The space between the logs was chinked, or stuffed, with pieces of wood. Daub was smeared over the chink. Just like the earliest homes, the chink and daub kept rain, wind, snow, and animals from getting inside. It wasn't long before smooth planks were used for floors and wall paneling.

By the 1700s, some of the newer houses were pretty fancy. Brick houses were owned by the rich. Some of the brick houses and even the wooden houses of the northern colonies had large porches, also known as **verandas**. A veranda could also be an enclosed porch on an upper level of a house. Now, that's fancy.

# Make Your Own

The colonists' trip to America took two or three months by sea on large ships. The ships could be about 100 feet long. These ships had to carry enough supplies for the long journey. Some of those supplies were food and water, clothing, guns and gun powder, tools and candles. The colonists brought the things they would need for their new lives with them. In this activity you can make your own ship and see if it floats or sinks.

**1** Take the wrapper off the bar of soap. Place the tracing paper over the soap.

**2** Using a pencil, draw an outline of a boat onto the soap through the tracing paper. The paper will keep the soap from getting pencil marks on it.

## Supplies

| | |
|---|---|
| ivory soap | potato peeler |
| tracing paper | other various |
| pencil | brands of soap |
| popsicle or | bucket or sink |
| orangewood stick | filled with water |

**3** Remove the tracing paper and carefully carve over the lines with a popsicle stick or orangewood stick. The stick acts like a knife but is much safer.

# SOAP BOAT

**4** Have an adult help you smooth the edges with a potato peeler. What a nice boat!

**6** Now, take your Ivory soap boat and place it in the water. Does it sink or float? Do you know why? It's because Ivory soap has air whipped into it. The air bubbles in the soap help it to float.

**5** Now find out if soap floats or sinks. Do you have a guess before you get started? Fill a bucket or sink with water. Take the wrappers off the other bars of soap. Place the bars one at a time into the water. What happens?

## Ben Said

⬦⬦⬦⬦⬦⬦⬦

**"Early to bed, early to rise, makes a man healthy, wealthy, and wise"**

This means you should get a good night of rest and an early start to do well the next day.

# Make and Eat

Log cabins were popular homes built by colonists from Ireland, Scotland, and Germany. Many of these settlers moved away from the coast in the 1700s into the mountains. Log cabins could be built in a few days and did not need any nails. Metal for nails was very expensive and not always available. Are you wondering how the houses stayed together without nails? The logs had notches cut at the end. When the logs were stacked on top of each other, they locked into place.

**1** Spread paper towels out on your work surface. Make a rectangle using four pretzel rods. Using a plastic knife, scoop out some vanilla icing and spread it on the pretzel rods. Stack four more pretzel rods on top of the icing.

**2** Keep making layers of icing and pretzel rods until your log cabin is as tall as you want it. About four or five layers is a good size.

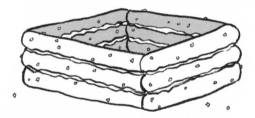

## Supplies

| paper towels | graham crackers |
| --- | --- |
| pretzel rods | mini chocolate chips or gumdrops |
| plastic knife | |
| vanilla icing | |

**3** Take two graham crackers and spread icing on the edges of them. Stick them together, forming a peak as the roof of the log cabin. Repeat this until the roof goes all the way across the cabin.

**4** Take one mini chocolate chip or gumdrop and spread icing on it. Stick it to a single graham cracker to make the door knob.

# A LOG CABIN

**5** Spread icing on the back of the graham cracker door and stick it to the front of the log cabin.

**6** Now it is time for the best part. You get to clean up by eating your log cabin. Yum!

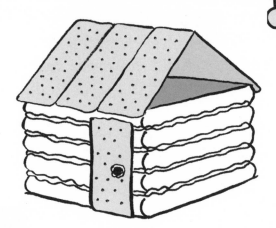

## Hey!!! it's Dark in Here

The colonists did not have electricity like we do. When it got dark they had two choices. They could go to sleep for the night or use candles for light. Families used a lot of candles in a year. Candles were made by the ladies of the village in large quantities several times a year.

Candle making was hard work. It also smelled bad because candles were made from animal fat. Sometimes they used oils or berries in the mixture so the candle would smell nice when it was used. The candles had to be dipped and dried and dipped again. The process was repeated over and over until the candles were a good size.

# Make Your Own CANDLE

The colonists did not have television or video games. In the evening the father often read the Bible to the family by candlelight. Here is an easy way to make your very own candle. You'll need to have an adult help you with some of the steps in this project.

**1** Sort through some broken crayons and remove the wrappers. Separate the crayons by color.

**2** Tie an 8-inch piece of string or candle wick to the pencil. Place the pencil across the top of a clean baby food jar.

**3** Have an adult help you melt the wax using a special microwaveable wax bag. Follow the directions for the time needed to melt the wax. The wax will be very hot! Please be careful.

**4** Place a broken crayon into the baby food jar. Have an adult pour some wax over the candle. The crayon will melt from the hot wax and make a spiral pattern.

**5** Add another piece of crayon, either the same color or a different color. Then pour more wax over this crayon. Layer the crayon and wax mixture until the jar is almost full. Let the candle harden.

**6** Clip the pencil off the string or wick after the candle hardens.

## Supplies

broken crayons
pencil
string or candle wick
baby food jar

white wax in microwavable wax bag
scissors

# Food
## Anybody Got a Net?

Can you imagine traveling all the way from England and having to gather and hunt and grow your own food in an unfamiliar land? Well, that's just what happened to the colonists. There was plenty of food around, but learning how to get it took some time.

The settlers were afraid to hunt in the forests for many reasons. The forests were thick with trees, and full of dangerous animals. Wolves and bears lurked in the woods and scared them. The colonists were also afraid of the Native Americans. Although many Native American people were friendly, others were not happy to see the new settlers moving onto their land. Some Native Americans had bad early experiences with European explorers, and fought the colonists.

Many of the crops the colonists planted did not grow well in this country. The climate and growing seasons were different from England. The berries and fruits that grew wild in America, such as cranberries and blueberries, were unlike what they'd seen before.

In the beginning the colonists didn't know what was safe to eat. They even struggled to catch fish. It was a tough time. When the winter months came along there was even less food. Many colonists did not survive their first winter in the New World.

# The Pilgrims

The **Pilgrims** were a group of colonists who settled Massachusetts beginning in 1620. Many Pilgrims were **Puritans** who came to America so they could worship freely. For years they had been persecuted in England for their religious beliefs. Not all of the Pilgrims were Puritans though. Like a lot of colonists, many came for the opportunity to start a new life.

WORDS TO KNOW

**Pilgrims:** people who came from England in the 1620s to settle Massachusetts. Some of the Pilgrims were Puritans.

**Puritans:** a group of people that came from England to Massachusetts to gain religious freedom.

**Tisquantum:** the name of the Wampanoag who helped the Pilgrims, who they called Squanto.

**Wampanoag:** the native American tribe of Tisquantum that lived in the area where the Massachusetts colony was founded.

**spiritual:** religious.

**trencher:** a piece of wood hollowed out and used instead of a plate.

The first Pilgrims came on a ship called the *Mayflower*. They arrived late in the year and had very little time to prepare for the winter. It was a difficult first winter for them and more than half died from the cold and lack of food.

Luckily a man named **Tisquantum** helped them. The settlers called him Squanto. He was a **Wampanoag** man.

**J**UST FOR LAUGHS

**Q:** What's the most musical part of a turkey?

**A:** The drumstick!

## Thanksgiving Fun!

**H**ave you ever wondered what the harvest feast that came to be known as the first Thanksgiving was like? It must have been like a party. The Pilgrims hunted birds like turkey and geese, and the Wampanoag brought five deer. Fruit was gathered and vegetables were prepared. There was plenty of food, talking, playing, music, and cleaning up afterwards.

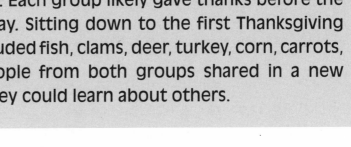

Both the Pilgrims and the Wampanoag people were **spiritual**, but in different ways. Each group likely gave thanks before the meal in their own way. Sitting down to the first Thanksgiving meal might have included fish, clams, deer, turkey, corn, carrots, and onions. The people from both groups shared in a new experience where they could learn about others.

In the spring Squanto taught them how to plant and raise corn because the English wheat did not grow well in Massachusetts. Squanto saved the lives of the Pilgrims. In 1621, the pilgrims of Plymouth, Massachusetts celebrated their good harvest with a feast—the first Thanksgiving!

Many of their new allies, the Wampanoags, joined them for the three-day celebration. They gave thanks to God for the help the Wampanoag people gave them.

## SPOTLIGHT ON MASSACHUSETTS

- Massachusetts was settled in 1620 by the Pilgrims. They sailed from Plymouth, England, on a ship called the *Mayflower*.

- In 1636 Harvard College was founded in Cambridge, Massachusetts, for colonial and Native American men. It was the first college in the New World. Harvard was named for a minister who left the college all of his books.

- *The Boston News-Letter* was the first newspaper in the colonies. It had short articles on what was going on in England, religious essays, and ship schedules. Isn't that interesting? Even though many colonists left England because they weren't allowed to follow their religious beliefs, they still liked knowing what was happening there.

- Fishing was an important business.

## Pull Up a Stool

The earliest colonists didn't have time to make furniture. Their dinner tables were very simple. Wooden planks on top of two barrels was a common table.

Family members sat on stools or benches. If there weren't enough seats, the children ate their meal standing. The few chairs were used by the men. They didn't have forks in those days, so people ate with spoons or knives—and their hands!

The knives had pointed ends for spearing food. Men and boys put their cloth napkins over their shoulders.

## THEN & NOW

| | |
|---|---|
| Legend says that the Pilgrims landed on a rock they called Plymouth Rock in Massachusetts in 1620. | Today a 10-ton boulder called Plymouth Rock gets one million visitors every year at the Pilgrim Memorial State Park in Plymouth, Massachusetts. The legend lives on. |

**Trenchers** were squares of wood with hollows carved into their centers. The hollows acted as plates. The wood was sanded smooth so they wouldn't get splinters in their food. Trenchers and wooden plates and cups were used until the 1850s in parts of America. Some families had plates and cups made out of clay or a metal called pewter.

In the early days most homes were just one-room cottages. The fireplace was the kitchen, and it heated the house too. Meals were cooked in a cast-iron pot with a handle hanging from above the flames of the fire.

Settlers made their own furniture, which took time. They built cradles for their babies, and their own chairs and benches. Where do you think they slept? At first they slept on the floor on mattresses filled with straw. Later they built bedframes, called bedsteads. The rich slept on mattresses filled with feathers.

19

Most colonial children had to share a bed with their brothers and sisters. They often slept in a trundlebed, a low bed that rolled out from under another bed. How would you like that?

As villages grew the colonists added on to their homes to make them bigger. Soon many homes even had an upper floor with several bedrooms.

## What's for Dinner?

What the colonists ate depended on where they lived. Those living near the ocean might eat crab or clams for dinner. Sweet potatoes grew very well in North Carolina and South Carolina. So colonists who lived in those areas might make sweet potato pudding, sweet potato pancakes, or have sweet potatoes with butter.

## COOL FACT

By the 1630s, the first gristmills were built in Virginia, Massachusetts, and other colonies. Mills were used to grind corn and grain into cornmeal and flour. This was much faster than grinding by hand. Here's how it worked: Mills were built next to a stream. A large wooden wheel would turn from the water flowing over it. That turning wheel was connected to a grinding stone inside the gristmill, and transferred the power of the water to the grinding stone. The grinding stone would mash the corn, wheat, or oats into flour. By 1649, Virginia had over 10 mills.

Apples grew better in the northern colonies. Colonists brought apple seeds with them from England in the mid-1600s. They would make applesauce and apple butter. They could also just grab an apple from a tree and eat it.

Corn did not grow in England, but the colonists learned how to plant and grow corn from the Native Americans. They had to teach the colonists how to cook with corn too.

The Native Americans also taught the settlers hunting techniques and showed them good places to hunt. Deer, bear, rabbit, squirrel, raccoon, and beaver were common animals that were hunted or trapped and cooked for food. The colonists kept livestock too, including cows and pigs.

What are your favorite foods? Do you know where those foods grow best?

## SPOTLIGHT ON NEW HAMPSHIRE

• An area that is now New Hampshire was first explored in 1614 by Captain John Smith—the same man who built a colony in Jamestown, Virginia, in 1607. The colony was founded in 1629.

• Dartmouth College was founded in 1769 by Reverend Eleazar Wheelock in Hanover, New Hampshire. It was open to colonists and Native Americans. It was important to Wheelock that all young men be able to receive a college education.

• Sawmills, cabinetmaking, and shipbuilding were important businesses in New Hampshire during colonial times.

• Farming was the most common job of the colonists in the area.

# Recreate Your Own COLONIAL FEAST

The first feast of thanksgiving between the Pilgrims and the Wampanoag tribe in 1621, in Plymouth, Massachusetts, lasted three days. That sure was a lot of celebrating! Their feast included turkey, duck, deer, fish, carrots, onions, beets, and corn. The activities listed in this chapter can become part of your own Thanksgiving feast. Don't forget to give thanks and clean up when you are done with the party!

## Supplies

Johnnycakes (recipe below)

cornstick muffins (recipe below)

colonial butter (recipe below)

rock candy (recipe below)

applesauce, juice, syrup, pretzels

cups, plates, napkins, forks, knives, and spoons

## COOL FACT

Sugar is a common ingredient that we use all the time. In colonial America though, sugar was an expensive luxury. At first it had to be imported from England. Later it was grown by slaves on many of the islands in the West Indies. These are some of the islands in the Caribbean Sea. Either way sugar came to the colonies by ship over long distances.

Sugar came in solid, cone-shaped loaves. If you wanted to use some sugar for a recipe you had to cut off a lump with a sugar nipper and grind it up before you could measure it out.

# Make Your Own
## JOHNNYCAKES

Native Americans showed the colonists how to cook with corn. Cornmeal pancakes, called johnnycakes, were a treat enjoyed by all. It took a lot of hard work to grow the corn, harvest it, and grind the corn into cornmeal. Do you think the hard work made the Johnnycakes taste extra good? Here is an easy recipe that can be made with a little help from an adult. Try adding some of the tasty stir-in ideas for variety.

## Supplies

stove

2 cups cornmeal

1 cup hot water

pinch of salt

2 tablespoons sugar

mixing bowl

wooden spoon

stir-in extras: raisins, chocolate chips, cranberries, blueberries

butter

frying pan

applesauce or maple syrup

**1** Add the cornmeal, hot water, salt, and sugar into a mixing bowl. Stir with the wooden spoon. Mix in one or more stir-in extras.

**2** Let the mixture sit for about half an hour, then form the mixture into eight flat pancakes.

**3** Melt 1–2 tablespoons butter in a frying pan over medium-high heat. Fry the Johnnycakes in the butter until golden brown on both sides. Enjoy with butter, applesauce, or syrup!

## COOL FACT

Have you ever heard someone call a kitchen "the heart of a home?" The kitchen in your house is probably a busy place. Well, the kitchen was even busier in colonial times. From cooking meals to making candles, from boiling water for baths and laundry to warming damp laundry by the fire, something was always going on there.

# Make Your Own
## COLONIAL BUTTER

We can easily buy butter in the grocery store today. It wasn't that easy for the colonists. Since the first cows were brought to America in 1623, they did not have butter before that. Once cows arrived, the colonists had to milk the cows and turn the milk into butter in a butter churn. A butter churn had a long handle with paddles on one end that was pushed up and down in a wooden container. After a lot of pushing the paddles up and down in the churner, the milk would begin to separate into a liquid and chunks. The chunks were the butter. The liquid was the whey. The liquid could be poured off, leaving the butter behind. You can make butter too.

## Supplies

container of heavy whipping cream | glass jar with a lid

| pinch of salt

**1** Pour heavy whipping cream into a glass jar, about half full. Tighten the lid on the jar. Shake the jar back and forth. Keep shaking! Take turns with a friend if you get tired.

**2** After lots of shaking, chunks will start to form. Keep shaking until the liquid starts to separate from the chunks. Pour off the liquid. Rinse the chunks of butter under water.

**3** Add the butter back into the jar and stir in a pinch of salt. Your fresh butter will taste great on your Johnnycakes. Refrigerate what you don't eat right away.

# Make Your Own
## CORNSTICK MUFFINS

Corn was a big part of the lives of the Native Americans. They would grind corn into a fine meal for cooking, or roast it. You can make corn muffins that look like corncobs. If you don't have a corncob pan use a regular muffin pan and cook for a few less minutes. Make sure you have an adult to help you with this activity.

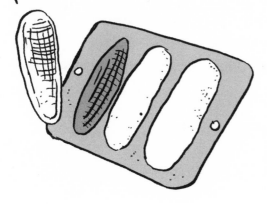

## Supplies

oven
cornstick pan
vegetable shortening
mixing bowl
mixing spoon
1 cup cornmeal
1 cup flour
⅓ cup sugar

2 teaspoons baking powder
½ teaspoon salt
1 egg, beaten
¼ cup vegetable oil
1 cup milk
toothpick

**1** Preheat the oven to 400 degrees Fahrenheit (200 degrees Celsius). Grease the cornstick pan with the shortening.

**2** In a large bowl, mix together the cornmeal, flour, sugar, baking powder, and salt. Add the egg, oil, and milk, and stir gently to combine. Spoon the batter into the prepared cornstick pan.

**3** Bake for 15 to 20 minutes, or until a toothpick inserted into the middle comes out clean.

# Make Your Own

Later in the colonial period, rock candy was a favorite treat of colonial children. They could buy rock candy at a general store or make it at home with their parents. This is a fun science experiment that can be eaten too! Since this activity requires pouring hot liquid, make sure you have adult supervision.

## Supplies

1 large pot

1 small pot

water

stove

4 clean glass jars, 1 pint each

cotton string

scissors

4 popsicle sticks or pencils

paper clips

granulated sugar

cup of water

food coloring

**1** Fill a large pot with water and boil. Sterilize the glass jars and paper clips by boiling them in the water for several minutes. Carefully remove and let dry.

**2** Cut four pieces of cotton string slightly longer than the height of the jar. Tie each piece of string to the center of a popsicle stick or pencil.

**3** Attach a paper clip to the other end of each string. Wet the string and pull it through the sugar so the string is coated with sugar. Set aside.

**4** Boil 1 cup of water in the small pot and add 2 cups of sugar. Stir to dissolve the sugar. Add a few drops of food coloring.

**5** Pour the sugar mixture evenly into each jar. Carefully lower the paperclip end of one string into one of the jars. The paperclip will keep the string from curling up. Rest the pencil or popsicle stick across the top. The string should not touch the bottom or the sides of the jar.

# ROCK CANDY

**6** Repeat with the remaining jars. Let the mixture sit for several days or even a couple of weeks to allow the sugar crystals to form. When finished, remove the rock candy from the jars. Let it dry for about 1 hour.

**7** You'll know it's ready to eat when the sugar crystals harden into small rock-shaped chunks. Don't worry—rock candy doesn't taste like rocks. It's yummy!

## Colonial Chocolate!

Do you like chocolate? Well, the colonists did too, but they had to order it from England. Chocolate was very expensive until they started making their own in the colonies. Newport, Rhode Island, had the first chocolate factory in the colonies. It was run by Obadiah Brown in 1752. Sadly, Brown only stayed in business long enough to make about 400 pounds of chocolate.

The second chocolate factory was started by John Hannon and Dr. James Baker in Dorchester, Massachusetts. Hannon had learned the secrets to making chocolate while living in Europe. In 1765 they started the Baker Chocolate Factory. It was a huge success with the colonists. Because the chocolate was made in the colonies, it was cheaper than ordering it from England. Finally, the colonists could afford to have a sweet tooth. Baker chocolates are still made today in Dorchester, Massachusetts.

# Plant Your Own
## HERB GARDEN

Many colonists had an herb garden that was separate from the flowers and vegetables they grew. This was called a "dooryard garden." It was usually near a door that got plenty of sun. It was handy to have herbs close to the house to use in cooking. Basil and oregano (they called it wild marjoram) were added to cooked foods for extra flavor. Herbs like peppermint were used as medicine for stomachaches. Lavender was dried and used in the house to make it smell nice. You can grow your own herbs just like the colonists did.

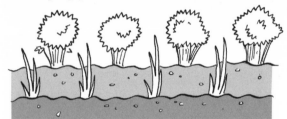

## Supplies

| empty, pint-sized milk cartons | potting soil herb seeds |
|---|---|

**1** Wash and dry a few empty, pint-sized milk cartons. Open the top of each milk carton. Fill halfway with potting soil.

**2** Take 3 or 4 herb seeds and plant them in the soil. Cover the seeds with a little more soil and water lightly. Repeat with the other herbs.

**3** Place the cartons near a sunny window. Water every few days. In a few weeks you'll have lovely plants that can be used for cooking or making a room smell nice.

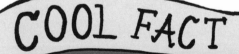

### COOL FACT

Do you like pizza? Dried basil, oregano, and thyme are spices used on top of pizza. Try planting those herbs for a pizza garden. Your homemade pizza will taste great with the fresh herbs you grew all by yourself!

# Native People

**N**ative Americans lived all over America for thousands of years before the colonists arrived. There were many different groups or **tribes**. Native Americans today use the word nation instead of tribe. The different nations spoke over 500 different languages! Each had unique art, beliefs, stories, and ways of living their lives.

---

Stories and traditions were passed down **orally**. Telling stories of their **ancestors**, of their beliefs and practices, was their way of teaching their culture and way of life to their children. What are some stories that you have learned from your grandparents about your family history? How does your family pass down traditions?

### Quick Colonial "quote"

*"Observe good faith and justice towards all Nations. Cultivate peace and harmony with all"*

~ *George Washington*

This means the colonists should be honest, fair, and peaceful with all people, from all countries.

Native Americans shared similar beliefs about nature. They felt their place was in the balance of nature, that they were caretakers of the earth. This meant they believed all humans should live alongside animals and not rule over them.

They were grateful for the food they received from nature and gave offerings to the Creator—the one who put them here on this earth—as a way of saying thank you. Festivals of thanksgiving were held many times a year. The purpose was to ask and thank the Creator for successful crops, as well as to thank the Creator for all that they received. While tribes did not always get along with each other, for the most part they lived peacefully in harmony with nature.

When explorers arrived from Europe it forever changed the lives of Native Americans. Some Europeans treated the natives as slaves. The explorers brought sicknesses and diseases that the Native Americans had not seen before. **Smallpox** was the worst disease for the Native

## COOL FACT

A branch of the Boy Scouts of America, the Order of the Arrow, is based on the teachings of the Lenni-Lenape peoples. These scouts show superior camping and wilderness skills, respect for nature, and a desire to teach others an appreciation for the land.

Americans because their bodies could not fight it. Sometimes entire villages died.

Some of the other deadly diseases were whooping cough, scarlet fever, typhoid fever, yellow fever, and diphtheria. Millions of Native Americans died as a result of contact with the Europeans. The languages and cultures of those who died were sometimes lost with them. Luckily many cultures survived and their traditions are still passed on today.

# Colonists Arrive

British colonists came to America with **charters**. A charter was a special document from the King of England giving a group of settlers a large piece of land. But the Native Americans had lived here for thousands of years before the colonists. Do you think the king had the right to give away this land? Who really owned it?

Many of these settlers belonged to religious groups that the king did not like. While they wanted to come here to practice their own faith, it was also a good way for the king to get rid of people he viewed as troublemakers.

As more settlers came by ship, the Native Americans worried about their land and food sources. They could see the colonists weren't really interested in sharing the land with them.

**WORDS TO KNOW**

**tribe:** a large group of people with common ancestors and customs.

**orally:** spoken out loud.

**ancestors:** people from your family or country that lived before you.

**smallpox:** a disease that spreads from person to person. People no longer catch smallpox but it used to kill many people every year.

**charter:** a paper given by the King of England to groups of colonists giving them large amounts of land in the New World.

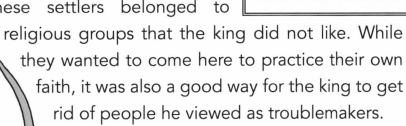

food

## SPOTLIGHT ON CONNECTICUT

• Connecticut was founded in 1635 or 1636 by Puritans looking for a place where they could worship freely.

• Farming and trading were important businesses in Connecticut.

• Noah Webster was born in West Hartford, Connecticut, in 1758. He published his first dictionary in 1806.

Sometimes the colonists and Native Americans quarreled, and these quarrels led to fighting. But many Native Americans were friendly and very helpful to the colonists. If it were not for the Native Americans teaching the colonists how to farm and where to hunt, most would not have survived.

Sadly, many colonists felt the Native Americans were **uncivilized** and treated them poorly. The colonists did not understand their different **customs** and beliefs. It's odd they judged the Native Americans so harshly. Many colonists had experienced misunderstandings about their own customs and beliefs.

## Come On Over to My House

The lives of Native Americans varied with the seasons. Many Native Americans lived in villages together for parts of the year. Their houses were not separated by yards or streets like we have today. Their homes were very near each other.

The land where they hunted, collected fruits and nuts, and farmed was not just the area right around their houses.

**uncivilized:** crude, not very advanced.
**customs:** way of life.

# Native People

The land they used covered very large areas. Where they hunted for deer, for example, could be more than a day's walk away. They might travel quite far to where they fished in the spring.

There were many styles of Native American homes. The style depended on where the tribe lived. When we think of Native American homes we usually think of **tipis**. A tipi is similar to a tent because it uses poles and a covering to enclose it. Most tipis were covered with either thin layers of bark from a tree or animal skins. It could be rolled up and moved easily when the village needed to move to an area with more food. Tipis were used by tribes living in the western part of America.

Another type of Native American home, called a **longhouse**, was an **oblong**-shaped home that several families shared. Longhouses were covered with wide sheets of bark. These homes were the most common in the eastern part of America, used by the **iroquois** people.

**tipi:** a house similar to a tent that uses upright poles and a covering to enclose it.

**longhouse:** an oblong house for many families.

**oblong:** a stretched-out rectangle with round corners.

**iroquois:** a group of five (now six) tribes in the area that is now New York state and Canada.

## COOL FACT

The word tipi has several spellings and all of them are correct. You can spell it tepee, teepee, or tipi. The women in the tribes made the tipis, set them up at the villages, and took them down when the group moved to a new place.

A typical longhouse might have enough room for 10 families. Sixty people could fit inside. Even larger longhouses could hold over 150 people, but they were not as common.

Families had separate sections to sleep in, and each had their own cooking area. Are you wondering how they all got along? Since this was their way of life,

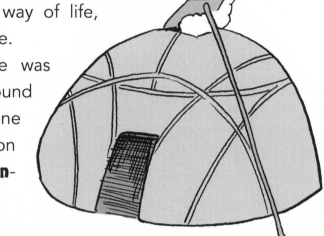

they normally got along just fine.

Still another type of home was called a wigwam. These were round houses. They were smaller, for one family. Wigwams were common with the northern **Algonquian**-speaking tribes.

WORDS TO KNOW

**Algonquian:** a large group of hundreds of tribes that lived in Canada and America, east of the Rocky Mountains. They spoke languages that were related.

**canoe:** a thin boat with pointy ends.

**toboggan:** an Algonquian word meaning sled.

**snowshoes:** lightweight frames shaped like tennis racquets worn on each foot. Snowshoes help you walk on top of deep snow.

## Can You Canoe?

Traveling by river to fish, hunt, or trade was made easy with a **canoe**. Making the canoe was a bit harder, though. It was a big job to chop down a large tree and hollow it out with fire. When the dugout canoe was finished some could hold more than 30 people. You may have seen pictures of a traditional canoe with one or two people in it. That style was called a birchbark canoe because it was made with bark from a birch tree. This type of canoe was more common in northern areas of Maine and Canada.

A birchbark canoe was made with sheets of bark shaped around thick strips of wood. The bark was sewn together with cedar roots to make it strong. This kind of canoe was light enough for one man to carry. It was fast in the water. Native Americans were very skilled in moving their canoes quickly through the water.

Traveling by foot was the main way to get about, but not always the fastest. When winter dumped snow and made travel difficult, the Native Americans used **toboggans** and **snowshoes** to get around. A toboggan is a long, narrow sled, with the front curved upward.

## THEN & NOW

Many towns in America took names that were originally used by the Native Americans.

Those names are still used today. They include those for the Maryland towns of Chicamuxen, Pomonkey, and Nanjemoy.

They could be 10 feet long. These sleds helped hunters bring food back to the village.

Snowshoes were used by men when they went out hunting. They were made from strips of wood shaped into a large oval with a strap that slipped over the person's leather moccasins.

Horses became the best form of transportation. They were brought to the East Coast by Europeans around 1639. They allowed Native Americans to travel faster to hunting areas, and to transport goods and supplies for trading. Because Native Americans had such respect for all life, they looked at these magnificent creatures as a blessing for assisting their lives so greatly.

## Baskets and Food

Baskets were very important in Native American life. They were used to carry food from the field or the river back to the village, and as containers to store food. Did the Native Americans get their baskets from the store? No, they made them!

They used thin strips of bark in different shades to add color to the designs They also used strong plant fibers such as **hemp**.

**COOL FACT**

The Inuit Indians, or Eskimos, are Native Americans who live in the far north of the Arctic region. They live in **igloos** made from blocks of snow.

These materials were woven into patterns and sewn together tightly with different materials, including **sinew**.

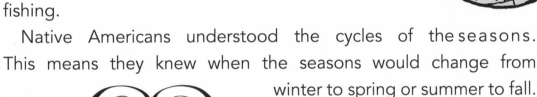

When the baskets were finished they could hold great amounts of weight.

The baskets were woven very tightly and were very strong. In areas to the west baskets were even used to carry water. Those same basket-weaving skills were used to make some mats, clothing, traps, and nets for fishing.

Native Americans understood the cycles of the seasons. This means they knew when the seasons would change from winter to spring or summer to fall.

## SPOTLIGHT ON RHODE ISLAND

• Rhode Island was settled in 1636 by Roger Williams. He built the town of Providence with the help of the Narragansett tribe.

• Roger Williams wrote a "dictionary" of the language of the Narragansett.

• Like many Native Americans, the Narragansett liked to hold archery (bow and arrow) competitions, and have races.

• Farming and fishing were important in Rhode Island.

• Fur trading between the Native Americans and colonists of Rhode Island was common.

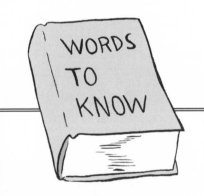

WORDS TO KNOW

**igloo:** a dome-shaped house made from blocks of snow.

**hemp:** a plant with strong fibers that Native Americans used to make baskets and rope.

**sinew:** a strong, thin band in an animal's body that connects bone to muscle.

They would often relocate to areas that had food or fruits that were coming into season. After gathering enough food for the winter they would move back to their winter village.

Native Americans were skilled at living off of the land. The Iroquois often lived near rivers and caught fish like salmon, herring, or trout. They used spears or nets with handles. Larger nets strung across a river allowed them to collect a lot of fish at one time. The Iroquois also gathered berries and nuts, and hunted.

Tribes that lived near the ocean, such as the Wampanoag and Narragansett, might eat clams, lobsters, and crabs. Many groups traveled to a river or the ocean at times of the year when fish were more plentiful. They would roast or dry their catches, then take the fish back to the village to be stored and eaten later.

Planting crops was an important part of life too. Corn was a major food source for the Native Americas. The Iroquois planted corn, beans, and squash together. These plants were called the Three Sisters because when they are planted together they get along.

## COOL FACT

Wampum was the name given to beads, necklaces, belts, and bracelets that Native Americans made from shells. The shells were mostly white, with purple to create designs. Wampum could be used as a message to another tribe. Or a beautiful necklace could be given as a present. When the colonists began trading with the Native Americans, wampum became a form of money used by the colonists.

The beans grow and climb up the tall corn stalks. The squash grows below the corn and beans and has huge leaves that keep moisture in the ground. The squash also helps keep weeds from growing. Succotash—a dish of cooked corn and beans—was very common. The women did most of the planting and harvesting. The men were the hunters.

## Ben Said

◇◇◇◇◇◇◇◇◇◇

**"A quarrelsome man has no good neighbors."**

This means if you argue with lots of people you won't have any friends.

# Hunting and Trapping

Native Americans were skilled hunters and trappers. They used spears or a bow with arrows. Arrow and spear points were made from stone, shell, or bone to hunt moose, elk, deer, ducks, geese, and turkey. The men trapped foxes, rabbits, beavers, raccoons, and squirrels. They would take the game back to the village where the women prepared the meat and skins.

Nothing was wasted. The bones were used for tools, weapons, or utensils. The claws and teeth were often used in jewelry, or to decorate clothing. Animal skins with the fur left on were used as warm blankets and to make heavier winter clothing.

Making animal skins soft enough for clothing was a long and difficult process called tanning. Usually the women tanned the animal hides by scraping off the fur and soaking, drying, and stretching the skins many times. The finished piece is leather. Leather was used mostly in bags and clothing.

# Make Your Own
## CLAY POTS

Some Native Americans made beautiful clay pots with designs on the outside. They used cords or sticks to print a pattern. There were several ways to make a clay pot. One common method was to mold the clay into thin rolls and place one coil on top of another to form a pot or bowl. The rolls would then be smoothed out. Pots were then printed with designs, hardened in a fire, and cooled. In this project you can make a clay pot and print or paint it too.

**1** Start by spreading newspaper on your work surface. Remember to wear a smock to protect your clothes.

**2** Try rolling the clay into long, thin pieces and coiling them around into the shape of a cup or bowl. Or work a clump into a ball and hollow it out. You could even mold the clay around a cup for the shape and slip the cup out when finished. Paint the pot if you like or etch patterns with the toothpick. Let it dry and harden.

## Supplies

newspaper | washable paint
smock | paint brushes
modeling clay | toothpicks

**3** There are many ways to make and decorate clay pots. Use your imagination and discover your own design!

# Make Your Own
# WAMPUM NECKLACE

In this project you can design, make, and paint your own wampum.

**1** Spread newspaper on a table or desk. Wear a smock to keep your clothes clean. Pour the paint into small paper cups or on an artist's palette.

**2** Measure a length of yarn around your neck that can be easily slipped on and off. Put the pasta into separate bowls by shape. Paint the pasta shapes and let them air dry.

## Supplies

| | |
|---|---|
| newspaper | yarn or string |
| smock | elbow macaroni, penne pasta, wagon wheels or other pasta shapes |
| washable paints | |
| small paper cups or an artist's palette | bowls |
| scissors | paint brushes |

**3** When the pasta is completely dry, string the shapes onto the yarn or string. You'll need to hold the other end of the string so they don't slide off.

**4** You can design a pattern using different shapes, or use just one type. After the yarn is full of your wampum, tie the two ends together.

## COOL FACT

Wampum is still made today. You can see wampum beads, necklaces, or belts on the following websites:
www.home.cshore.com/waaban/wampum.html
www.mohicanpress.com/wampum_bead_prices.html
www.crazycrow.com/

# Hold Your Own
## TRADING POST DAY

The colonists and the Native Americans traded food, furs, and other supplies using wampum as money. You can have a Trading Post Day and use the wampum you just made to buy fun items. Here are a few suggestions to get you started:

## Supplies

| | |
|---|---|
| wampum | music CDs |
| erasers | granola bars |
| pencils | juice boxes |
| notepads | packs of gum |
| books | |

**1** Clear a table. Line up items to purchase: erasers, pencils, notepads, books, music CDs, granola bars, juice boxes, and gum. Use the wampum you made to buy the items.

**2** Trading means you have to agree on a price. How many packs of gum is a wampum necklace worth?

# Clothing and Wigs

**W**hen the colonists first settled the New World, there were no stores selling clothing. They brought clothes with them from England, but what happened when clothing wore out or children outgrew their clothes? The colonists either had to make their own or order more from the supply ships.

Supply ships from England took several months to arrive with clothes, tools, food, and other needed supplies. As more people came to live in the New World, blacksmiths, candle makers, wig makers, and leather makers started new businesses in the growing villages.

The clothing the colonists wore was made to last a long time. Adults and children were dressed pretty much the same way.

The children looked like small grown-ups wearing the same type of clothing as their parents. Men and boys wore **breeches**. with long white stockings that came up to their knees. Men also wore white shirts and a vest, and a long coat over the vest. Shoes had buckles rather than laces or Velcro. As a boy outgrew his clothes they were passed down to his brother.

**THEN & NOW**

| The latest fashion styles came from Paris, France. | Paris is still the center of the fashion world. |

Clothing for women and girls was very different from what we see today. Colonial women wore floor-length dresses with **stays**. Wealthy ladies began wearing gowns with **hoop skirts** underneath. The hoop skirt made the gown look very rounded and puffy. Sitting down on a chair was pretty hard. If the lady didn't sit down just the right way the hoop skirt would fling up in front of her face. That must have been embarrassing!

**WORDS TO KNOW**

**breeches:** tight-fitting pants that go to the knees.

**stays:** a stiff, tight-fitting vest worn under a dress.

**hoop skirt:** a garment worn under a gown to make it puff out.

**spinning wheel:** a wooden wheel with a foot pedal used to make thread out of cotton or wool.

**dye:** to make a color.

**loom:** a large machine that wove thread into fabric.

Many colonists made their own clothes. Fabric was woven from wool, cotton, or linen. Linen comes from the flax plant. The colonists needed to grow and harvest flax and cotton before turning it into thread to weave into fabric. Wool was gathered from sheep and spun on a **spinning wheel** into thread.

Girls were taught to spin. A spinning wheel is a large wooden wheel with a foot pedal that rests on the floor. As the girl pressed on the foot pedal the wheel spun. Holding the wool or flax between her fingers, the wheel pulled it and spun it into thread.

After it was washed and **dyed**, the threads could be woven on a **loom** into fabric. Looms were used to make cloth out of threads. Using different colored threads could create patterns on the fabric. Threads were woven in an under-and-over pattern and then pushed back tightly with a special tool.

## The King's Rules

Strangely enough, the colonists weren't supposed to weave fabrics or even have sheep. The King of England wanted them to send their thread to England to be woven into fabric there. Even though the colonists lived in the New World they still lived under British law. Why would the king care about cloth? This way the colonists would have to buy their fabric from England. In the 1700s the colonists imported more cloth from England than anything else. So the weavers in England made a lot of money selling cloth to the colonists. But many colonists felt this was unfair. Some kept sheep and wove their own fabric anyway. This is one example of how the King of England made laws that were difficult for the colonists to live with.

Many women had their own looms and made their own fabric. Eventually weavers came to the New World and set up weaving shops. Many colonists still spun their wool, cotton, and linen, but some chose to have weavers make the fabric. After the fabric was made the cloth was cut and sewn into clothing.

## Ben Said

"Guests, like fish, begin to smell after three days."

This means company gets annoying if they visit for too long.

By the 1700s, colonists had more money from trading furs, tobacco, cotton, or food. They could afford new clothes and even wigs. Hats, capes, and muffs became popular.

A cape was a long flowing coat. A muff was like a fur sleeve with two open ends that ladies put their hands into for warmth during cold days outside.

## Craftsmen and Trades

Craftsmen were trained in a certain **trade**. Sometimes they had helpers. These helpers could be **indentured servants**, **apprentices**, or even **slaves**.

## Indentured Servants

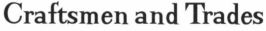

**M**any colonists could not afford the cost of travel from England. More than half came as indentured servants. Usually an indentured servant had to work for seven years for the person who paid their way to the New World. After that they were free to live and work where they pleased. Many indentured servants worked on the farms of wealthy landowners or in the small businesses of the towns.

**WORDS TO KNOW**

**trade:** a skill or business.

**indentured servant:** a person who travels to another country free in exchange for work to pay for that trip.

**apprentice:** someone training in a trade.

**slave:** a person owned by another person and forced to work without pay, against their will.

**custom made:** something made specially for a person.

Cobblers repaired shoes. New shoes were expensive, so cobblers stayed busy repairing worn out shoes for the colonists. Most shoes were made from leather. They were heavy, clunky shoes, not like the comfortable sneakers we have. Some shoes were made to be worn on either foot. No worrying about lefts and rights!

A tanner turned animal skins into leather. This was a long process of scraping, soaking, and washing. The leather was made into shoes, belts, bags, saddles, and buckets. A leather bucket may sound silly to us, but many colonial families owned one. These buckets were used to help put out fires since wooden buckets could burn.

Tailors made clothes for men and women. In colonial America, breeches, gowns, and coats were **custom made** for everyone, including slaves.

## SPOTLIGHT ON NEW YORK

• New York City was settled in 1624 by the Dutch colonists. They called the land New Netherland. When the British took over the area in 1664 they renamed it New York.

• The Iroquois Confederacy, a group of Native nations, was the main Native American presence in the area.

• Fur trading and shipping grain to Europe for sale were common businesses.

The difference between clothing for the wealthy and for the slave was in the quality of the fabric. Until 1675 tailors made gowns, but then gown making became a separate trade.

A milliner was a woman who owned a shop that sold fabric. She also sold imported fashion items such as gloves, hats, shoes, and jewelry. She made fashion accessories such as aprons, caps, cloaks, muffs, and trim for gowns. Milliners also mended clothing. Someone who made gowns was called a mantua maker. A milliner was often a mantua maker as well.

The wigmaker made wigs out of horse, goat, yak, or human hair. Wigs were a status symbol for the wealthy during colonial times—for both men and women. Some wealthy landowners even had their slaves wear wigs for important occasions. Wigs were often powdered and perfumed.

## Slavery

Many people were forced to come to America as slaves. Slaves were not free and could not earn their freedom. They were often prisoners from England or captured people from Africa bought by wealthy people. Many Native Americans were forced into slavery too. Children of slaves were automatically slaves and members of slave families were often separated when their owners sold them. Slavery in America began during colonial times in America and finally ended during the Civil War in 1865.

Especially in the south, many colonists owned large farms, called plantations. Cotton and tobacco were two crops grown on southern plantations. It took a lot of workers to run a plantation. Most plantation owners used indentured servants and slaves.

# COOL FACT

The Conestoga wagon was invented in Conestoga Valley, Pennsylvania, in 1730 by German settlers. This covered wagon had wide wheels that helped the wagon get through mud instead of getting stuck in it. The covering on the wagon protected the contents from the weather. It also offered shade to anyone going along for the ride. These wagons were big and needed six or more horses to pull them. By 1750, thousands of Conestoga wagons had been built. The wagons were used to transport goods to market in the towns and cities, as well as to transport settlers and their possessions to new territories.

A blacksmith was very important to a town. He made things out of iron, such as the pots that were used to cook meals, as well as horseshoes, nails, and tools. The cooking pots were used by both colonial and Native American women.

Furniture was made by cabinetmakers. They made chairs and tables and desks, as well as chests of drawers for clothing. Early colonial furniture was often simple and plain. As the wealth of many colonists grew, the demand for fancier furniture with more detailed carvings grew too. Most designs were similar to furniture styles from England.

# Quick Colonial "quote"

"Conscience is the most sacred of all property."

~ *James Madison*

This means that knowing right from wrong and being an honest person are the most important qualities you can have.

## COOL FACT

Many people who wore wigs were not bald, so when they were fitted for a wig their heads had to be shaved so the wig would fit snugly. But, after wearing these snug wigs they would begin to lose their hair.

Coopers were very important in colonial times. They made wooden barrels that could hold liquids without leaking. Barrels were also used to store corn, cornmeal, meat, and sugar. Coopers made barrels in different sizes and made buckets too.

Colonists bartered for what they needed. Bartering is another word for trading, without using money. Gold and silver coins were hard to get so trading was more common. Colonists also used wampum as a form of money.

Later each colony printed its own paper money, but colonists still preferred coins instead of paper.

### SPOTLIGHT ON PENNSYLVANIA

• Pennsylvania was settled in 1682 by William Penn. He was a member of the Society of Friends, a religious group also called Quakers. Quakers were and still are peaceful people.

• The Native American tribe called Lenni-Lenape live in this area. Manyunk, Conshohocken, and Neshaminy are just a few town names that come from the Lenape language.

• Philadelphia was an important port city designed by William Penn. It was meant to be a city that welcomed everyone. People of many cultures lived in and near Philadelphia.

• Sawmills, farming, and iron ore were successful businesses.

• Benjamin Franklin grew up in Boston, but considered Pennsylvania his home.

• The Declaration of Independence was signed in Philadelphia.

# Make Your Own
## COLONIAL WIG

Wigs became popular in Europe and then colonial America when King Louis XIII of France started wearing one to hide his hair loss. Wealthy men and ladies wore wigs even if they had hair. They were just trying to be in style. It was a lot of work to make a wig, so they were very expensive. Hair was curled and sewn into a cap that was specially made to fit the customer's head. The most formal wigs were white, with a ribbon tied in the back around a ponytail or braid. There were many styles of wigs to choose from.

**1** Put the beanie cap on. Stretch out a long piece of white quilting fluff. Tuck some of the fluff under the front of the cap. Use the bobbi pins to hold the fluff in place.

**2** Add to the fluff until the wig is the desired length. Take the cap off and glue the fluff to the underside of the cap. Let it dry.

**3** Place the cap back on. Flip the fluff up and over your head. Tie back the wig with a ribbon.

## Supplies

| old winter beanie cap | fabric glue |
|---|---|
| white quilting fluff | ribbons |
| bobbi pins | clips and decorations |

Have fun making different hairstyles with your wig. You can curl the "hair," add ribbons and other decorations, or pin you wig up into a fancy hairdo. Later you and your friends can have a tea party and dress up with your wig like the wealthy colonists did.

# Make Your Own
## TEA SANDWICHES AND HAVE A TEA PARTY

Wealthy colonists enjoyed tea, and often gathered to chat with each other at teatime. Have an adult help you assemble peanut butter and jelly sandwiches, chicken salad sandwiches, egg salad sandwiches, or cucumber and butter sandwiches. Cut the sandwiches into little triangles. Tea sandwiches are fancy because they have the crusts cut off the bread. Dress up in some fancy clothes. Put on your wig and have a party with these fun tea sandwiches.

### Supplies

whole grain bread

knife

peanut butter & jelly

cucumber slices

butter

chicken salad

egg salad

juice

hot chocolate

wig

fancy dress-up clothes

## COOL FACT

Children enjoyed playing with dolls in colonial times. Usually only rich children had real dolls. Families with less money might make corn husk or rag dolls. Paper dolls would have been very popular among colonial children because they are so cute. Try drawing pictures of Colonial Jane and Colonial John. From looking at the pictures in this book can you draw different outfits for your dolls that were common for their time? A girl's outfit would have a bonnet, white dress, apron, and shoes with a buckle. A boy's outfit would include trousers, a white shirt with large collar, and shoes with a buckle.

# Make Your Own POMANDER BALL

**Pomander balls were used by the colonists to make their house or a drawer smell good.**

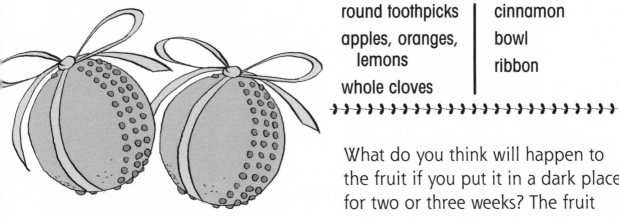

## Supplies

| | |
|---|---|
| round toothpicks | cinnamon |
| apples, oranges, lemons | bowl |
| whole cloves | ribbon |

What do you think will happen to the fruit if you put it in a dark place for two or three weeks? The fruit will harden and then it can be used for a long time to keep a closet smelling nice.

**1** Take a toothpick and poke holes into the fruit of your choice. You can make a design, or just make random holes.

**2** Push the end of a whole clove into each hole. Fill a bowl with cinnamon. Roll the fruit with the cloves around in the cinnamon.

**3** Tie a ribbon around the fruit to hang it, or place several in a bowl. Put the fruit in a dark, cool place for two or three weeks.

# School and Games
## Let's Learn and Play!

**S**chool and play time were very different for colonial kids compared to what children are used to today. Of course there were no video games or televisions. In fact, there weren't even any schools at first.

All children learned skills about daily life from their parents. The father often read the Bible to the family in the evenings. During the day, children worked very hard around the house and on the land. Boys helped build houses, chop wood, and plant crops. Girls helped with cooking, washed clothes by hand, sewed, and looked after younger brothers and sisters.

But like you, children and families did have time for some fun. In their free time the children played games like leapfrog and marbles.

## Public School

In 1635 the first public school was started in Boston, Massachusetts. The school was called the Boston Latin School. Samuel Adams, Benjamin Franklin, and John Hancock all went to Boston Latin. They were important during the American Revolution. This was the war that the colonists fought against England for independence. Each of these men signed the Declaration of Independence.

They rolled hoops and flew kites. People living in the New England colonies enjoyed ice skating on a frozen pond or playing in the snow during winter months. Men often played darts or card games. Ladies would sit around a table and talk while working together on a quilt.

## Time for School

As more settlers came to the New World and villages and towns grew, school became an important part of a child's life. Like today, some schools were public schools where any child could attend, and others were expensive private schools. But the subjects studied, the length of the school day, and the amounts of days children attended school depended on the region they lived in.

The colonies were thought of as three very different regions. Do you know why? Because of the weather, the crops grown in those areas, and the religious groups that settled in them. Those three regions were called the New England colonies, the Middle colonies, and the Southern colonies.

The New England colonies were Massachusetts, New Hampshire, Rhode Island and Connecticut. The Middle colonies were New York, New Jersey, Pennsylvania, Delaware, and Maryland. The Southern colonies were Virginia, North Carolina, South Carolina, and Georgia. The regions had different types of schools. This was mostly because of the school locations.

### SPOTLIGHT ON DELAWARE

• Delaware was settled in 1631 by Dutch settlers.

• William Penn took over Delaware in 1681. Even though Penn had settled in Pennsylvania, Delaware was important because it was close to the ocean for trading.

• Tobacco was grown by many farmers in Delaware.

• Fishing was an important business in Delaware.

## New England

Puritans lived mainly in the New England colonies. Remember, this strict religious group left England because they were not allowed to follow their faith in England. They came to the colonies to be free to worship in their own way. They believed in a simple, hardworking life devoted to God.

## COOL FACT

The first textbook in the colonies was called the *New England Primer*. It was published in 1690 in Boston. The book was for older children. Rhymes helped children learn their letters. It also had prayers, the Ten Commandments, and other religious readings in it. Children learned their prayers and to read at the same time.

**Delaware was the first colony to fly the colonial flag.**
**The flag had 13 stars on it to stand for the 13 colonies.**

Puritans promoted education to further their religion. All of their daily activities were centered around their beliefs. Their faith was also a very big part of what children were taught in their schools.

Private schools were expensive and for older boys only. Boys learned foreign languages and were taught to read the Bible. Girls were not allowed to attend.

Town schools for both girls and boys were similar to the elementary schools that we have today. Children learned the basics of reading, writing, and arithmetic (math) in these one-room schoolhouses There was only one teacher for all of the children, who were ages 5 all the way up to age 14. The teacher would often work with the children according to their age levels. Kids that were over 14 who did not go on to private school could train with a tradesperson to prepare for a job.

Q: Why is the math book so sad?

A: Because it's full of problems!

## Middle Colonies

People with many different religions lived in the Middle colonies. Because there were so many different beliefs, each church usually held their own school in the church during the week.

One religious group living mainly in Pennsylvania was the **Quakers**. They had their own schools, too, that taught reading, writing, and math, as well as farming and craft skills. The Quakers were very peaceful and did not believe in beating children. Other schools of the colonial era punished naughty children by beating them.

**Quakers:** a peaceful religious group.

**tutor:** a teacher who gives private lessons.

## Southern Colonies

There were very few schools in the southern colonies because people lived on large plantations and their homes were far apart. Wealthy southerners hired **tutors** to teach their children at home. Poor southern children and slaves generally did not learn to read and write.

### SPOTLIGHT ON NEW JERSEY

• New Jersey was settled in 1664 by British colonists.

• Wheat grew well in New Jersey. It became a common crop grown and traded by the colonists.

• Many Lenni-Lenape lived in the area. These Native Americans lived in wigwams and paddled canoes to get from place to place along the many rivers of the region.

• Trenton was a busy city in New Jersey.

## Music

Many families in the colonies sang songs and played music. The most common instruments were the banjo, flute, and fiddle. A fiddle is the same as a violin. They are called different names depending on the music and the way the instrument is held.

## THEN & NOW

| In colonial times children in some areas went to school six days a week from 7:00 a.m. to 5:00 p.m. | Kids have weekends off from school and are finished with their day by 3:00 p.m. |

The songs they sang were ones they knew from England. Many songs were church hymns. Church choirs became popular in the New England colonies.

In the Middle colonies there were Irish and German settlers and the busy Philadelphia port in Pennsylvania bringing in people from other countries. Colonists from the Middle colonies had the opportunity to hear music played by several different cultures.

The Southern colonists may have been influenced by Spanish settlers. The slaves there made songs to sing while they worked in the fields. They sang about the struggles in their difficult lives and their faith. Their songs were rich in passion and came from their hearts. These types of songs later influenced blues and gospel music.

The mix of cultures and music made an impression on the colonists. Even though it was not until the late 1700s that the colonists began creating their own style of music, the colonial period is where it all started happening.

**Connecticut is the home of Yale University—the third oldest college. It was named after Elihu Yale, who donated a lot of money to the school.**

## COOL FACT

In 1620, the colony of Virginia built the first library in the New World. The colonists donated their own books to be shared by others in the village.

## Gatherings

Even though the colonists worked very hard, they still knew how to have fun. They turned difficult work into community events that involved neighbors helping each other. After the work was finished they shared in the fun part—eating, dancing, and relaxing. Some of these events were cornhuskings, barn raisings, and quilting bees.

Cornhusking involved a community picking and peeling many baskets of corn. When they were done the neighbors could all take some home with them. When the next neighbor needed his corn picked and husked everyone would all come back and do it again. A barn raising took several days. A group of men would help build a barn for a neighbor while the ladies cooked together. Then everyone would share the meal.

Quilting bees involved the women and girls in the community. Quilts are large, cozy blankets made of lots of pieces of fabric sewn together. Women helped each other make beautiful quilts for their homes. It was a chance for the women to accomplish a large task while enjoying each other's company. The younger girls watched and helped out as part of their training.

# Make Your Own HORNBOOK

Hornbooks were the books colonial children used in school. A hornbook was really just a paddle with a paper attached to it. The paper might have a prayer and the alphabet on it. There were few real books available in the New World at first. Hornbooks were practical and kids could focus on just the one page. The name comes from the clear, very thin layer of cow's horn that covered the paper to protect it. The horns were boiled and sliced so thin that you could see through it, like a layer of clear plastic. The paddles were made from wood or ivory. In this activity you'll make a hornbook. What will your hornbook say?

**1** Draw the shape of a paddle or square with a handle on cardboard. The paddle should be a bit larger than your piece of paper. Cut out the paddle.

**2** Write the alphabet, numbers, a prayer, or a poem on the piece of paper. Place the paper on the paddle, but not on the handle.

## Supplies

cardboard         paper
pen or marker      clear plastic wrap
scissors           tape

**3** Carefully put the plastic wrap over the paper and smooth it out. Fold it neatly over the edges of the cardboard to the back of the paddle. Tape the plastic wrap to the back.

# Make Your Own
## MARBLES

Marbles were a popular game played by colonial children. The most common marble game was called ring taw. Four to six children would play it together. Marbles were made from colorful glass or clay that was baked in a fire.

## Supplies

newspaper

smock

air-drying modeling clay

washable paint

paint brushes

**1** Spread newspaper on a table. Put a smock on to protect your clothes. Squish and knead the clay following the package directions.

**2** Take small pieces of clay and roll them into round balls to make individual marbles, all about the same size. Make 10 small marbles and one larger marble for each child. The larger marble could be the size of two small marbles put together.

**3** Let the marbles air dry. Paint the marbles in fun colors if the clay is white.

**4** Play ring taw with your marbles. There are lots of variations of the game, but the simple version on the next page is a fun way to start.

# Play
## RING TAW

**1** Take the string and make a circle about 10 inches wide. Tie the ends of the string together so the circle doesn't come apart when you play.

**2** Each player places some of their marbles in the center of the ring. If you have lots of players then each can put three marbles into the ring. If you have just a couple of players then each can put seven or eight marbles into the center.

**3** The large marble is called the shooter marble or taw. The first player places their shooter on their thumb with the thumbnail under the index finger. The goal is to flick the shooter at the marbles in the ring, trying to knock marbles out of the ring.

## Supplies

| | |
|---|---|
| string | marbles |
| scissors | 2-6 friends |

**4** The shooter wins any marbles that roll out of the ring and gets to go again. If the player doesn't knock any marbles out of the ring then it's the next player's turn. When all of the marbles have been knocked out, the player with the most marbles wins. You can also make teams for ring taw.

# Make Your Own

Corn husk dolls originated with the Native Americans, and both Colonial and Native American children played with these dolls made from dried corn husks. This activity requires an adult because it is complicated.

## Supplies

bags of cornhusks (found at craft stores or farmer's markets)

bucket of water

string

scissors

yarn for the hair

glue

cloth scraps for clothing

**1** Soak the cornhusks in a bucket of water so they are soft. Take four cornhusks and arrange them as shown.

**2** Using a small piece of string, tie the straight ends together tightly. Trim and round the edges with scissors.

**3** Turn upside down and pull the long ends of the husks down over the trimmed edges. Tie with string to form the head.

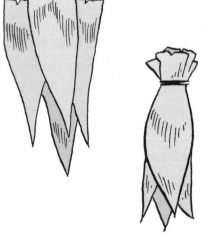

# CORN HUSK DOLL

**4** Take another husk, flatten it, and roll into a tight cylinder. Tie each end with string. This forms the doll's arms.

**5** Fit the arms inside the long husks just below the neck. Tie with string, as shown, to form a waist.

**6** Drape husks around the arms and upper body in a criss-cross pattern to form shoulders.

**7** Take four or five husks, straight edges together, and arrange around the waist. Tie with string.

**8** If you like you can form legs with small strips of husks. Finish off the doll by tying small strips of husk around the neck and waist to hide the string.

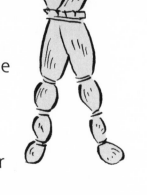

**9** Glue yarn to the head for hair. You can glue and tie small scraps of cloth to the doll for clothing.

# Famous People

**What's Your Name?**

**J**ust who were some of these people who lived during colonial times? They were like Americans today—regular people trying to live a good life. But they bravely ventured into the unknown by leaving England and Europe to come to the wilderness of the New World. They worked hard to build new homes and new lives here.

---

The villages and colonies grew. Soon America began to seem like its own country to the colonists, separate from the Old World. Eventually the colonists fought the Revolutionary War for independence from England. Many made great sacrifices for this independence. The leaders of the time created our system of government, which today allows us to live our life freely.

Some of the colonists were very well known because of something special they did in their lifetime. Let's meet a few of these people!

# In the Beginning

**Captain John Smith** was the leader of the colonists that came to Jamestown, Virginia. He helped the settlers build a village there in 1607. During a fight between the Powhatan tribe and the village, John Smith killed two of the Native Americans. John Smith was captured and taken to the chief.

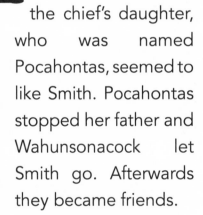

Chief Wahunsonacock planned to have John Smith killed for what he had done. But the chief's daughter, who was named Pocahontas, seemed to like Smith. Pocahontas stopped her father and Wahunsonacock let Smith go. Afterwards they became friends.

Returning to the settlers, Smith tried to organize the colonists to gather food. But many of them were more interested in searching for gold.

## SPOTLIGHT ON VIRGINIA

• Captain John Smith settled Virginia in 1607.

• Tobacco was grown by many colonists, who became very wealthy selling it to England.

• Slaves were often used as workers on tobacco farms.

• Chief Wahunsonacock was the powerful leader of many Algonquian-speaking tribes called the Powhatan Confederacy.

• The city of Williamsburg was made the capital of Virginia in 1700.

Smith realized he had to get their attention, and he told the settlers "He who does not work, will not eat." That got them moving.

The village and the settlers thrived. John Smith was injured in an accident in 1609 and returned to England for medical treatment. Sadly, Jamestown did very badly without his leadership. The people ran out of supplies and many became sick and died. A few years later Captain Smith returned to America and explored New England and the area that would later become the colony of New Hampshire. He drew a map with English names for many of the Native towns, such as Plymouth. Smith was the one who named the region New England.

**Pocahontas** was the daughter of the Powhatan chief, Wahunsonacock. When Pocahontas was 10 or 11 years old she saved Captain John Smith's life by stopping her father from having Smith killed. Pocahontas and Smith were friends. She often played in Jamestown with the colonists' children.

By 1610 the friendship between the colonists and the Powhatans was not going very well.

## THEN & NOW

In 1630 there were 5,000 settlers living in the New World. By 1760 the population had grown to 1,500,000 colonists living in the colonies.

Today there are over 300 million people living in the United States. That's quite a lot more people!

**poet:** someone who writes poems.

**poem:** creative writing that has a rhythm and sometimes rhymes.

## SPOTLIGHT ON NORTH CAROLINA

• Colonists from Virginia began to settle in North Carolina in 1653.

• Many Cherokee Native Americans lived in the area that the colonists called North Carolina.

• The Native American crops of tobacco and corn were the main crops in North Carolina.

• Blackbeard was the scariest pirate during colonial times. He robbed many ships and made his hideout in North Carolina.

Then Pocahontas married John Rolfe, a Virginia tobacco farmer, in 1614. Their marriage brought peace between the two villages. They traveled with their baby Thomas to England where Pocahontas met the queen. Sadly, Pocahontas got smallpox and died before she could return to Virginia.

**Anne Bradstreet** was the first colonial **poet**. Anne was a Puritan. She moved to Massachusetts from England with her husband and children. Bradstreet enjoyed reading and often read to her children. She wrote **poems** about the difficult life of a Puritan colonist and her love for her children and husband.

Her only book of poems was published in 1650. Bradstreet's brother had read her poems and liked them. He knew his sister was talented. He borrowed the poems and had them made into a book under her name without her knowledge.

Here are a few lines about nature from one of her poems:

Under the cooling shadow of a stately elm
Close sat I by a goodly river's side,
Where gliding streams the rocks did overwhelm.
A lonely place, with pleasures dignified.
I once that loved the shady woods so well,
Now thought the rivers did the trees excel,
And if the sun would ever shine, there would I dwell.

**Roger Williams** was kicked out of Massachusetts by the Puritans. The Puritans were very strict and often punished people for disobeying their rules. Williams believed that the church should be separate from the government. This is called separation of church and state. So he traveled alone by foot to the area where Rhode Island is today. Williams became friends with the Narragansett tribe and learned to speak their language.

The Narragansett people liked Williams because he traded with them honestly.

**JUST FOR LAUGHS**

**Q:** How do trees get on the Internet?

**A:** They log in.

## Border Dispute

The colonies of Maryland and Pennsylvania disagreed on their boundaries. So they hired surveyors named Charles Mason and Jeremiah Dixon to figure out a boundary that everyone could live with. The Mason-Dixon line became the official boundary line between Maryland and Pennsylvania in 1767. This line was important later, because after the American Revolution it was used to decide where slavery was allowed. South of the Mason-Dixon line, slavery was legal. North of the line people could not own slaves.

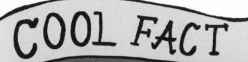

Benjamin Franklin invented a musical instrument called the glass armonica. The player used foot pedals that moved glass bowls. As the bowls turned the player would wet his finger and touch the bowls to make them hum. It made a most interesting sound.

He told them about his religion, but understood they had their own beliefs. The Narragansett helped Williams start his settlement in 1636, which he named Providence. Soon other peaceful settlers joined Williams in his town where people could observe any religion.

## Later in Colonial America

**William Penn** founded Pennsylvania in 1682. He was a Quaker. Quakers believe in spreading peace, truth, and love to all. They do not believe in violence. Penn knew that there were many Lenni-Lenape living in the area that became Pennsylvania. He wrote a letter to chief Tamanend, explaining that he wanted to live there and that he was an honest man. The chief agreed.

Penn made plans for a city with a port for ships. He named the city Philadephia. That means the "city of brotherly love." Philadelphia welcomed people of different faiths who wanted to live in a peaceful land.

**Benjamin Franklin** was a very wise, funny man and is considered a great American hero. He was trained as a printer by his brother. In 1729 he bought a newspaper called the *Pennsylvania Gazette*. Franklin was the printer and also wrote many of the articles in the newspaper. In 1733 he started writing and printing *Poor Richard's Almanac*.

This book told farmers about the weather. It also had prayers and recipes in it. In addition to all of his other interests, Franklin was an inventor. He created swim flippers, bifocal reading glasses, a stove to warm houses, and many other inventions as well. Benjamin Franklin was the oldest man at 70 years old to sign the Declaration of Independence.

**Ben Said**

"Speak little, do much."

This means stop talking and do your work.

**Phyllis Wheatley** was the first African American colonist to publish a book. She was a slave whose owners taught her to read and write. Wheatley wrote a book of poems called *Poems on Various Subjects, Religious and Moral*. It was published in 1773. She became famous when she mailed a poem to George Washington while he was at war. He liked her poem so much that he sent it to *Pennsylvania Magazine* so that it could be published for all to read. She earned her freedom with her poetry. You can visit a statue of her at the Boston Women's Memorial.

## SPOTLIGHT ON MARYLAND

• The first settlers arrived in Maryland in 1634. Maryland was founded by Lord Baltimore of England. The city named after him is Maryland's largest city.

• St. Mary's City was the first settlement and a popular place for colonists to live because it was near the Chesapeake Bay. Fishing was an important business.

• Four men from Maryland signed the Declaration of Independence. They were William Paca, Charles Carroll, Samuel Chase, and Thomas Stone.

# Make Your Own
## COLONIAL JOURNAL

In colonial times, many people lived in rural areas on farms. Everyone spent a lot of time outside. What can you find outside if you go for a walk? Do you see pretty stones and leaves? How about squirrels, rabbits, and birds? If you splash through a stream can you find polliwogs or snakes? Go out for a walk with your parents and explore! Even if you live in the city you can get out into nature in a park. Look around and you'll find all kinds of treasures to bring home. You can make a journal and write a story with pictures showing the fun you had outside.

## Supplies

| | |
|---|---|
| small pocket-sized notebook | foam shapes or letters |
| treasures from a walk | paint and paintbrush |
| glue | colored pencils |

**1** First decorate the cover of your journal. Use some of the treasures you collected, such as leaves, pebbles, moss, or an unusual piece of bark. Play with the arrangement to decide what you want to use and where you want to put each item.

**2** Glue the pieces onto the notebook. You can use the foam shapes dipped in paint to make a design or write a word. Let everything dry.

**3** Using the colored pencils, draw pictures of your nature walk. Write a story telling about your experience to go with the pictures. Can you write a poem about something you noticed?

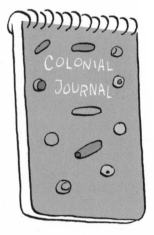

# Make Your Own
## STATIC ELECTRICITY TEST

Benjamin Franklin discovered electricity in 1752 by flying a kite during a **lightning** storm. That might sound like a silly thing to do, and it was, because it was very dangerous. Ben thought that thunderstorms and electricity had something to do with each other. So he tried an experiment. During the storm, lightning struck a key on the kite and Ben received a shock. Ouch! His experiment worked, and it gave him another idea. Ben invented the **lightning rod**, which protected houses from being hit by lightning and catching on fire. You should never, ever try Ben's experiment. But you can play your own game to discover **static electricity**.

**WORDS TO KNOW**

**lightning:** a flash of static electricity during a storm.
**lightning rod:** a metal rod attached to the highest point of a building that attracts lightning and guides it to the ground.
**static electricity:** electricity made by rubbing two different objects together.

**1** Blow up several balloons. Try to stick them on the wall. What happens?

**2** Now, rub a balloon on your hair for a moment and try again. When you rub the balloon on your hair you create static electricity and the balloon sticks to the wall.

**3** Now try another experiment. Shuffle around on a carpet in your stocking feet. Rub your feet on the carpet with each step. After a few minutes the static electricity will build up on your body.

**4** Touch someone. Feel the shock? You are passing the electricity to them.

# Make Your Own
## SCAVENGER HUNT

**Colonial children enjoyed scavenger hunts. A scavenger hunt is a game played to find a list of items. You can have a scavenger hunt with some friends using some of the items you've read about in this book or made from the activities in book!**

**1** Divide into two groups. Divide the items you will search for into two groups as well. Each group will hide their items in a different room.

**2** Write questions or clues for each item to be hidden. An example could be, I'm used as money for trading food and supplies. What am I? (Answer: wampum). This way each group has to figure out what they are looking for AND find it.

**3** Now hide your items. It's fun to find hiding places where the item blends into its background, so it's right there but hard to see.

## Supplies

| | |
|---|---|
| marbles | paper doll |
| candles | hornbook |
| corn husks | pomanders |
| cornhusk dolls | paper |
| wampum | pencils |
| clay pots | notebook |

Clue #1

**4** Once each group has hidden all of its items the two groups exchange clues and starting playing. The first group to find everything wins.

**5** Have prizes for the person who answers the most questions correctly, or finds the most items.

75

We have already learned that many colonists came to this country to have a better life. Many of them came to worship in their own way. Some were hoping to find gold. Others heard that the New World had plenty of good farmland. The crowded countries in Europe did not have land for everyone. Still other colonists came for the adventure. What an adventure it was!

Whether the settlers came from England or other European countries, they still thought of themselves as belonging to their homelands long after they arrived. But many years of struggle and trade helped the colonists feel that they were part of something new and exciting.

That "something new" was feeling united as a group of people building something out of nothing. At times British settlers worked alongside Native Americans, Dutch settlers, German settlers, and Irish settlers. England and Europe were far away from the New World.

**THEN & NOW**

| Traveling over oceans could only be done by ship. | Today most people fly over oceans in airplanes. |

They didn't forget their homelands, but they started viewing themselves as a new group of people. They were beginning to see the 13 colonies as a nation, or a country of its own. The British colonists felt this way more than others because the king make their lives so hard.

The **French and Indian War** was the beginning of a new outlook for the colonists. The war lasted seven years, from 1756 to 1763. The British soldiers from England fought with the British colonists against the Native Americans and the French. They were fighting for control of the New World, for the lands that stretched all the way from Georgia to Canada. England won the war.

## SPOTLIGHT ON GEORGIA

• Georgia was the last of the 13 colonies to be settled. It was started in 1733 by James Oglethorpe.

• The Cherokee and Creek were the main Native American tribes in the area. Hart, Georgia was the "assembly ground" for the Cherokee peoples. They held council meetings and conducted trading in this place. A boulder now marks the place of Ah-ye-li-a-lo-hee or Center of the World as it was called at the time.

• Cotton and rice were the most common crops grown in Georgia.

WORDS TO KNOW

**tax:** an extra charge put on a product by the government. The government gets the extra money.

**boycott:** refusing to buy products to protest something.

**Sons of Liberty:** group of angry colonists who took action against King George III.

**protest:** strongly disagree with a person or idea.

**Boston Tea Party:** the name given to the dumping of tea into Boston Harbor to protest the tax on tea.

The war cost England a lot of money. The king of England decided the colonists should pay for it. He charged the colonists extra for many items that came from England, such as tea or clothing. The extra charges were called **taxes**.

Of course the colonists didn't like this one bit. They were mad. They said the taxes were not fair. The colonists complained to King George III, but he didn't care. He just kept charging them more and more. Many colonists stopped buying items that were taxed, such as sugar and tea from England. This is called a **boycott**.

## Boston Tea Party

Some colonists from Boston, Massachusetts, started a group called the **Sons of Liberty.** The leaders of the group were John Hancock and Samuel Adams. The group took action against the taxes. The action was called a **protest**.

The Sons of Liberty valued symbols. The Mohawk tribe was viewed as a group that stood up for their beliefs, and the Sons of Liberty liked that. So in 1773 the Sons of Liberty dressed up in Native American clothing, imitating the brave Mohawks, and climbed onto boats in the harbor carrying supplies. They dumped over 300 boxes of tea into Boston Harbor. It was called the **Boston Tea Party**. It wasn't really a tea party, though. It was a strong protest sending a strong message. The Sons of Liberty did this to show King George III how mad they were about his taxes.

What do you think the king did when he found out that over 300 boxes of his tea were ruined and not paid for? If you guessed he was mad, you're right! The king was so mad that he made a law to punish those tea-dumping colonists. Of course, he didn't really know which colonists dumped the tea, so his new law punished all of the colonists.

He actually made several laws, and they were called the Intolerable Acts. These new rules really made the colonists mad. First the Boston port was closed so that ships could not get in to bring supplies or take goods to sell to England. The port would only be opened if the colonists paid for the damaged tea.

**The colony of New York was named after the Duke of York, in England.**

Another law said that the British soldiers in Boston could live in a colonist's home, and the colonists had to feed them. Well, that did it. Now the colonists were really mad at the king. With each new tax and law the colonists became braver and more **rebellious**. They started saying no to the king more often. King George III was running out of options. He planned a secret attack in Massachusetts against the colonists.

Somehow his plan was discovered. Paul Revere and two other colonists rode horses at night on April 18, 1775 from Boston to Concord, Massachusetts, to warn the colonists of the attack. Up and down the streets they swiftly rode yelling to the colonists that the British were coming.

## Quick Colonial "quote"

"All men having power ought to be distrusted to a certain degree."

~ *James Madison*

This means that someone in charge might be more interested in staying in charge than doing the right thing.

Paul Revere was captured but when the British attacked the next day the colonists were ready. The reason we remember Paul Revere so well is because of the poem, "Paul Revere's Ride," written by Henry Wadsworth Longfellow. The poem starts with the words:

**"Listen my children and you shall hear
Of the midnight ride of Paul Revere"**

**Over 100 battles took place in New Jersey during the Revolutionary War.**

## THEN & NOW

| | |
|---|---|
| The Declaration of Independence was signed on July 4, 1776. It was a very important document. | It is still a very important document. See it for yourself at the National Archives Museum in Washington, DC. |

The poem helped make Paul Revere famous. The British attack on April 19, 1775 is considered the beginning of the **Revolutionary War.** It is also the end of the Colonial era and the beginning of the Revolutionary era. The war lasted from 1775 to 1783. George Washington was the leader of the American soldiers in the war.

# Declaration of Independence

Congress was the name of a group of colonists that met in Philadelphia, Pennsylvania, to discuss problems the colonies were having. They decided it would be a good idea to explain to all of the colonists why independence was important. People needed to understand why a war with England was necessary.

Many colonists had these ideas already, but they hadn't taken a stand as a nation before. Benjamin Franklin, John Hancock, Samuel Adams, Thomas Jefferson, John Adams, and others met in Philadelphia to talk about their ideas.

## WORDS TO KNOW

**rebellious:** fighting against authority, or those in charge.

**Revolutionary War:** the war the 13 British colonies fought with England for independence. It lasted from 1775 to 1783.

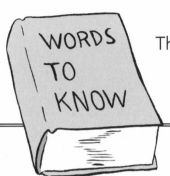

They asked Thomas Jefferson to put their ideas into writing because he was a good writer.

The paper he wrote was called the **Declaration of independence**. Thomas Jefferson worked hard for two weeks putting these ideas on paper. When he was finished it was read to Congress. Jefferson's words were powerful, and Congress liked it. Congress signed it on July 4, 1776. Today we celebrate July 4th as Independence Day. The men who signed the Declaration of Independence are called our Founding Fathers. They helped explain what America stands for and declared our independence from Great Britain.

**Declaration of independence:** the paper that Thomas Jefferson wrote explaining what America stands for.
**ivory:** the material that elephant's tusks are made of.

## What Did It Say?

The Declaration of Independence said that all people living in the colonies had certain rights. Some of those rights were to have a good life, live in a free country, and be happy. It also said the colonists were no longer British people. They were members of a new country called America!

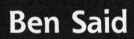

### Ben Said

⬦⬦⬦⬦⬦⬦⬦⬦⬦⬦

"He that lieth down with dogs shall rise up with fleas."

This means if you hang around with bad people their behavior will rub off on you.

## Founding Fathers

So, who were our Founding Fathers? The Founding Fathers were the 56 men who signed the Declaration of Independence. They were the voice of a beginning America.

Some of the Founding Fathers were quite famous. You've already met Ben Franklin, but let's meet some others now.

**George Washington** did not actually sign the Declaration of Independence because he was busy leading the Revolutionary War. But he agreed with all of the ideas of Congress. Washington was a skilled leader. He was very brave and cared about his soldiers. He made a lot of surprise attacks on the enemy that helped win the war. When the war was over George Washington was elected our first President.

## COOL FACT

It was always thought that George Washington had false teeth made from wood. He did have false teeth, but they were made from **ivory.**

**Samuel Adams** was a very good speaker. He lived in Boston, Massachusetts. Adams told the people in his town that the British were wrong to put high taxes on products they bought from England. He wrote articles in the *Boston Gazette* newspaper explaining his thoughts. Adams started the Sons of Liberty group to go against the taxes of King George III. He gave his ideas to Thomas Jefferson when he was writing the Declaration of Independence.

**John Hancock** is known for having the largest signature on the Declaration of Independence. He was the first person to sign the document. His large signature was on purpose, to show that he was not afraid to stand up for what he believed was right. Hancock was from Boston, Massachusetts, and one of the leaders of the Sons of Liberty. He wanted the colonists to be free from the rule of England. This was very important to him. Hancock was a rich man who used a lot of his own money to help pay for the Revolutionary War. He gave many ideas to Thomas Jefferson for the Declaration of Independence. Sometimes people will say "Put your John Hancock here." That term refers to your signature because John Hancock was so famous for his signature.

**Thomas Jefferson** came from a wealthy family in Virginia. He grew up to become a lawyer. Jefferson is famous for a lot of things, and one of them is his home, called Monticello. You can visit Monticello. He is also famous for writing the Declaration of Independence.

## SPOTLIGHT ON SOUTH CAROLINA

• South Carolina was settled in 1663 by the British, but it was part of North Carolina at first. South Carolina became a separate colony in 1729.

• The Cherokee Path was a footpath that led to all neighboring Cherokee areas in South Carolina. It was a common way used during trading.

• Charleston was a busy city with a port for ships. It was originally called Charles Town.

• Rice and indigo were important crops in South Carolina. Indigo is a plant used to make a dark blue dye. The settlers sold the dye to trading ships.

The men in Congress knewhewoulddoagood job writing the beliefs of our young country. He used a feather pen when he wrote the Declaration of Independence. Jefferson later became our third President. After he retired from politics he helped start and design the University of Virginia.

**John Adams** was also important during the time of American's fight for independence from England. A lawyer from Massachusetts, Adams thought England was wrong to tax the colonists so much. He also thought the Boston Tea Party was a good idea. John Adams helped convince members of Congress to sign the Declaration of Independence. He later suggested that George Washington be in charge of the army at the start of the Revolutionary War. John Adams was America's first vice president, and our second President.

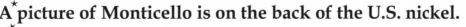

A picture of Monticello is on the back of the U.S. nickel.

# Make Your Own
## FEATHER PEN

The colonists wrote with feather pens. The feathers are called quills. These quills were cut at the bottom so a small amount of ink flowed onto the paper, just like a pen you might use today. The pen had to be dipped into the ink often to write a letter. Have an adult cut the feather quill.

**1** Spread newspaper on a table. Put a smock on to protect your clothes.

**2** Have an adult cut the bottom of the quill. It needs to be cut diagonally. Make a little slash at the tip of the feather.

**3** Pour some ink into a glass jar. Dip the feather pen into the ink. Dab the pen onto a paper towel to catch excess ink.

**4** Start writing a note on the paper. Dip the pen back into the ink as the feather pen starts getting empty.

## Supplies

| | |
|---|---|
| newspaper | ink |
| smock | small glass jar |
| sharp knife | paper towels |
| feather quills (found at craft stores) | paper |

**J**UST FOR LAUGHS

**Q:** Why did the man throw his watch out of the window?

**A:** He wanted to see time fly!

**Algonquian:** a large group of hundreds of tribes that lived in Canada and America, east of the Rocky Mountains. They spoke languages that were related.

**American Revolution:** the war fought by the colonists for freedom from Great Britain.

**ancestors:** people from your family or country that lived before you.

**apprentice:** someone training in a trade.

**barn raising:** a community event to build a barn for someone.

**Boston Tea Party:** the name given to the dumping of tea into Boston Harbor to protest the tax on tea.

**boycott:** refusing to buy products to protest something.

**breeches:** tight-fitting pants that go to the knees.

**canoe:** a thin boat with pointy ends.

**charter:** a paper given by the King of England to groups of colonists giving them large amounts of land in the New World.

**colonial America:** the name given to this country when talking about the years 1607–1776.

**colonies:** early settlements in America.

**colonist:** a person who came to settle America.

**corn husks:** the leaves that cover an ear of corn.

**custom made:** made specially for a person.

**customs:** way of life.

**daub:** clay mixture used to cover the wattle in between logs in colonial houses.

**Declaration of independence:** the paper that Thomas Jefferson wrote explaining what America stands for.

**dye:** to make a color.

**forest:** an area with lots of trees and wildlife.

**hemp:** a plant with strong fibers that Native Americans used to make baskets and rope.

**hoop skirt:** a garment worn under a gown to make it puff out.

**hornbook:** an early book that was in the shape of a square with one sheet of paper on it. The square had a handle at the bottom so it could be held and read easily.

**igloo:** a dome-shaped house made from blocks of snow.

**indentured servant:** a person who travels to another country free in exchange for work to pay for that trip.

**iroquois:** a group of five (now six) tribes in the area that is now New York state and Canada.

**ivory:** the material that elephant's tusks are made of.

**lightning:** a flash of static electricity during a storm.

**lightning rod:** a metal rod attached to the highest point of a building that attracts lightning and guides it to the ground.

**longhouse:** an oblong house for many Native American families.

**loom:** a large machine that wove thread into fabric.

**Native Americans:** the native people who already lived in areas settled by the colonists.

**New World:** what is now America. It was called the New World by people from Europe because it was new to them.

**oblong:** a stretched-out rectangle with round corners.

**orally:** spoken out loud.

**Pilgrims:** people who came from England in the 1620s to settle Massachusetts. Some of the Pilgrims were Puritans.

**poem:** creative writing that has a rhythm and sometimes rhymes.

**poet:** someone who writes poems.

**protest:** strongly disagree with a person or idea.

**Puritans:** a group of people that came from England to Massachusetts to gain religious freedom.

**Quakers:** a peaceful religious group.

**quilting bee:** a gathering of women to make a quilt together.

**rebellious:** fighting against authority, or those in charge.

**Revolutionary War:** the war the 13 British colonies fought with England for independence. It lasted from 1775 to 1783.

**settlers:** the brave men, women, and children who came from other countries to settle in the New World.

**sinew:** a strong, thin band in an animal's body that connects bone to muscle.

**slave:** a person owned by another person and forced to work without pay, against their will.

**smallpox:** a disease that spreads from person to person. People no longer catch smallpox but it used to kill many people every year.

**snowshoes:** lightweight frames shaped like tennis racquets worn on each foot. Snowshoes help you walk on top of deep snow.

**Sons of Liberty:** group of angry colonists who took action against King George III.

**spinning wheel:** a wooden wheel with a foot pedal used to make thread out of cotton or wool.

**spiritual:** religious.

**static electricity:** electricity made by rubbing two different objects together.

**stays:** a stiff, tight-fitting vest worn under a dress.

**tax:** an extra charge put on a product by the government. The government gets the extra money.

**tipi:** a house similar to a tent that uses upright poles and a covering to enclose it.

**Tisquantum:** the name of the Wampanoag who helped the Pilgrims, who they called Squanto.

**toboggan:** an Algonquian word meaning sled.

**trade:** a skill or business.

**trencher:** a piece of wood hollowed out and used instead of a plate.

**tribe:** a large group of people with common ancestors and customs.

**tutor:** a teacher who gives private lessons.

**uncivilized:** crude, not very advanced.

**veranda:** a large porch with a roof above it.

**Wampanoag:** the native American tribe of Tisquantum that lived in the area where the Massachusetts colony was founded.

**wattle:** sticks and straw filling the spaces between logs.

**wigwam:** a dome-shaped house made with bark covering a frame of saplings.

# Books

**Barretta, Gene.** *Now & Ben.* New York: Henry Hold and Company, 2006.

**Bordessa, Kris.** *Great Colonial American Projects You Can Build Yourself.* White River Junction, VT: Nomad Press, 2006.

**Burgan, Michael.** *Life in the Thirteen Colonies: Maryland.* New York: Scholastic, 2004.

**Burke, Davis.** *Getting to Know Jamestown.* New York: Coward, McCann & Geoghegan, 1971.

**DeFord, Deborah H.** *Life in the Thirteen Colonies: Massachusetts.* New York: Scholastic, 2004

**DeFord, Deborah H.** *Life in the Thirteen Colonies: Pennsylvania.* New York: Scholastic, 2004.

**Doak, Robin.** *Life in the Thirteen Colonies: Georgia.* New York: Scholastic, 2004.

**Doak, Robin.** *Life in the Thirteen Colonies: Massachusetts.* New York: Scholastic, 2004.

**Earle, Alice Morse.** *Child Life in Colonial Days.* New York: The McMillan Company,1930.

**Earle, Alice Morse.** *Home Life in Colonial Days.* New York: The McMillan Company,1965.

**Emily, Lauren.** *Life in the Thirteen Colonies: Connecticut.* New York: Scholastic, 2004.

**Fisher, Margaret and Fowler, Mary Jane.** *Colonial America English Colonies.* Michigan: Gateway Press, Inc., 1988.

**Fradin, Dennis.** *The Thirteen Colonies.* Chicago: Childrens Press, 1988.

**Heaton, Vernon.** *The Mayflower.* New York: Mayflower Books, Inc., 1980.

**Howath, Susan.** *Colonial People.* Brookfield, CT: Millbrook Press, 1994.

**January, Brendan.** *The Thirteen Colonies.* New York: Childrens Press, 2000.

**Kalman, Bobbie and Crossingham, John.** *Colonial Home.* New York: Crabtrees Publishing Group, 2001.

**Oberle, Nora Polack.** *The Declaration of Independence.* Minnesota: Capstone Press, 2002.

**McMaster, Gerald and Trafzer, Clifford E.** *Native Universe: Voices of Indian America.* Washington, D.C.: The National Geographic Society, 2004.

**Paulson, Timothy J.** *Life in the Thirteen Colonies: New York.* New York: Scholastic, 2004.

**Pobst, Sandy.** *Life in the Thirteen Colonies: Virginia.* New York: Scholastic, 2004.

**Pony Boy, GaWaNi.** *Horse Follow Closely.* California: Bow Tie Press, 1998.

**Samuel, Charlie.** *Entertainment in Colonial America.* New York: The Rosen Publishing Group, 2003.

**Samuel, Charlie.** *Home Life in Colonial America.* New York: The Rosen Publishing Group, 2003.

**Smith, Carter.** *Daily Life: A Sourcebook on Colonial America.* Brookfield, CT: Millbrook Press, 1991.

**Sterngass, Jon.** *Life in the Thirteen Colonies: New Jersey.* New York: Scholastic, 2004.

**Stevens, Peter F.** *The Mayflower Murderer & Other Forgotten Firsts in American History.* New York: William Morrow and Company, Inc., 1993.

**Tunis, Edward.** *Colonial Craftsmen.* Ohio: The World Publishing Company, 1965.

**Tunis, Edward.** *Colonial Living.* Ohio: The World Publishing Company, 1957.

**Worth, Richard.** *Life in the Thirteen Colonies: Delaware.* New York: Scholastic, 2004

**Worth, Richard.** *Life in the Thirteen Colonies: North Carolina.* New York: Scholastic, 2004.

**Worth, Richard.** *Life in the Thirteen Colonies: South Carolina.* New York: Scholastic, 2004.

**Wright, Louis B.** *Everyday Life in Colonial America.* New York: Putnam, 1966.

## Museums of Interest

**Colonial Williamsburg** www.history.org  Williamsburg, Virginia

**Frontier Culture Museum** www.fronteirmuseum.org  Staunton, Virginia

**Fort Delaware Museum of Colonial History** www.scgnet.us.org
Sullivan County, New York

**National Museum of the American Indian** www.nmai.si.edu
Washington, D.C. and New York, New York

**North Carolina Museum of History** www.ncmuseumofhistory.org
Raleigh, North Carolina

**The Metropolitan Museum of Art** www.metmuseum.org  New York, New York

**The National Great Blacks in Wax Museum** www.ngbiwm.com
Baltimore, Maryland

**The National Society of the Colonial Dames of America** www.nscda.org
Museum properties across the U.S.

## Websites

**Colonial Williamsburg** www.history.org

**David McHam's Communication Law Center** www.class.uh.edu

**Declaration of Independence**
www.ushistory.org

**eHow** www.ehow.com

**Encarta** http://encarta.msn.com/

**Family Fun Magazine** www.familyfun.com

**Federal Reserve Bank of Boston**
www.bos.frb.org/education/pubs/
historyo

**George Washington's Mount Vernon Estate & Gardens** www.mountvernon.org

**Iroquois Confederacy and the US Constitution** Portland State University
www.iroquoisdemocracy.pdx.edu

**Lenape Nation** www.lenapenation.org

**Library Think Quest**
www.library.thinkquest.org

**Motivational & Inspirational Quotes by Benjamin Franklin**
www.MotivationalQuotes4U.com

**MSNBC** www.msnbc.msn.com

**Native American Technology and Art**
www.nativetech.org

**Native Languages of the Americas**
www.native-languages.org

**Organic.org** www.organic.org

**Orrin Lewis** www.bigorrin.org

**Scholastic**
www.scholastic.com/scholastic

**Social Studies for Kids**
www.socialstudiesforkids.com

**The Association for the Preservation of Virginia Antiquities**
www.preservationvirginia.org

**The Claude Moore Colonial Farm at Turkey Run**
www.1771.org

**The Colonial Music Institute**
www.colonialmusic.org

**The Electric Ben Franklin**
www.ushistory.org

**The New England Unit of The Herb Society of America** www.neuhsa.org

**The Thirteen Original Colonies**
www.scarborough.k12.me.us

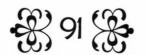